U.S. History

People and Events that Helped Build America

Contents

Author **Erin Ash Sullivan** earned a master's degree in education from the Harvard University Graduate School of Education. She has written numerous nonfiction books for children, including *The Seven Wonders of the World* and *Get Ready for Social Studies: U.S. History*. Sullivan teaches history and English at the Willows Community School in Culver City, California, where she is also an administrator active in developing curricula.

Consultant **James L. Alouf, Ph.D.,** chairs the Department of Education at Sweet Briar College in Sweet Briar, Virginia, where he is also a professor. He is the author of *American History Smart Junior: Exploring America's Past*. Dr. Alouf earned his Ph.D. in social studies from the University of Virginia.

Facts verified by **Barbara Cross.**

Louis Weber, CEO
Publications International, Ltd.
7373 North Cicero Avenue
Lincolnwood, Illinois 60712

Permission is never granted for commercial purposes.

ISBN-13: 978-1-4127-1358-0
ISBN-10: 1-4127-1358-7

Manufactured in China.

8 7 6 5 4 3 2 1

AMERICA'S BEGINNINGS

Native Americans and European settlers established homes and cultures and explored the North American continent.

When does the story of America begin? To find out, you'd have to travel back in time thousands of years to when Earth was in the middle of an ice age. Because much of Earth's water was frozen into glaciers, the sea levels dropped, and huge areas of land were no longer covered by water. Scientists call these areas land bridges. One land bridge was at the Bering Strait, up where North America is close to Asia. Between 10,000 and 30,000 years ago, early people traveled across this land bridge from Asia into North America.

THE EARLIEST AMERICANS

These first Americans were nomadic. That means they traveled from place to place, hunting animals and gathering plants to eat. Over many years, some groups of these people began to settle in small villages where they farmed the land.

From 1000 B.C. to A.D. 1300, people settled across North America. The Adena, the Hopewell, and the Mississippian Mound Builders lived near the Ohio, Missouri, and Mississippi rivers. Archaeologists are scientists who study ancient cultures. They learned that these early people grew corn, beans, and squash. The people created jewelry, weapons, and tools out of clay, stone, and metal. They also traveled far distances and traded with other groups.

These early people also built huge burial mounds, hundreds of feet long and almost 20 feet high. Some mounds were even in the shapes of animals, such as birds, bears, and buffalo. These people didn't have any known building tools, so how did they create such large structures out of earth? No one knows for sure.

The mammoth was an early ancestor of today's elephants. Mammoths roamed North America before they became extinct when the last ice age ended, about 10,000 years ago. One theory is that the mammoths died out because of the change in climate. Another theory is that they were overhunted by humans.

HOW DO WE KNOW?

How do scientists and archaeologists find out about early people? They examine ancient artifacts, or handmade objects, for clues. Old pieces of pottery, fragments of bone, and scraps of cloth can provide a lot of information about how people lived long ago.

Native American burial mounds

NATIVE AMERICAN CULTURES

Over time, the Mound Builders faded away, and new cultures developed across North America. From about 1300 to 1500, Native American nations created different kinds of shelter, transportation, and art, all depending on what natural resources were available nearby.

The Anasazi were an early group of Native Americans that lived in the Southwest. They created these petroglyphs, or "rock-writings," as a way to share information and stories.

The central part of North America was covered with wide grassy plains. There, peoples such as the Cheyenne and the Sioux relied on the buffalo for almost every part of their daily life. They ate buffalo meat and used buffalo hides to stay warm during the harsh winters. They also used buffalo hides to make their tipis, which were cone-shape homes that they could pick up and move easily from place to place while they hunted.

In the Southwest, the Navajo, the Hopi, and other nations struggled with a hot, dry climate and poor soil. They used their water resources carefully and grew corn, beans, and squash. The Hopi created rock homes by carving rooms out of steep cliffs, while the Navajo built hogans—round homes made of logs and covered with mud.

Along the Northwest Coast, the Haida, the Tlingit, and other cultures fished in the rough seas. They carved sturdy canoes out of tall, strong cedar trees. Planks from the cedars were also used to build their homes, called longhouses. Longhouses were very long, indeed: up to 100 feet long and 25 feet wide! Many relatives shared one longhouse. Each family's section was set apart by mats woven from cedar bark or cattail plants.

On the West Coast, peoples such as the Chumash enjoyed a mild climate and many food resources. They caught fish, hunted deer, and collected acorns. Their homes, called aps, were simple structures

THE VIKINGS

Many people think that the first European explorers in North America were from Spain and Portugal, but that's not correct. Believe it or not, the Vikings were here first! The Vikings were expert sailors who traveled far distances across the oceans. They established settlements in Greenland and Iceland, far from their homes in Northern Europe. Leif Eriksson was a Viking who traveled from Greenland to North America around the year A.D. 1000. His brothers tried unsuccessfully to start a settlement in Newfoundland, which is now part of Canada. Today, visitors can go to L'Anse aux Meadows Historic Site in Newfoundland, where archaeologists have uncovered remains of that early Viking settlement.

Plains tribes used buffalo hides for many things, including clothing and tipis. These Sioux women are preparing the hides by stretching them out on frames on the ground. After scraping off the hair, they would rub the hides with buffalo brains to make the hides soft and flexible.

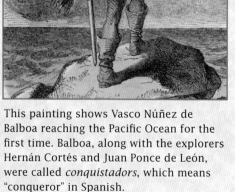

THE FOUR CORNERS
The "Four Corners" is a special spot in the southwestern United States where four states meet: Arizona, Colorado, New Mexico, and Utah. The Ute and Navajo Indians originally occupied this land, and some still live there.

Columbus was greeted as a hero when he returned to Spain. He shared the story of his adventures and showed off some native people who had joined him on the voyage home. He also introduced new wonders to the Spanish: turkeys, pineapples, tobacco, and a brand-new kind of bed called a hammock!

woven from grasses and easily remade if a storm or an earthquake toppled them.

The Eastern Woodlands Indians, such as the Iroquois and the Narragansett, used the forests as their main source of food and shelter. They hunted bear and deer, grew crops of corn, beans, and squash, and collected maple syrup. Some Eastern Woodlands nations built shelters called wigwams, which were sturdy structures covered in tree bark. Other nations built longhouses that were similar to the ones found along the Northwest Coast.

THE AGE OF EXPLORATION

Europe was changing rapidly in the 1400s. Artists were creating beautiful paintings, scientists were making new discoveries, and inventions such as the printing press were changing life forever. Europeans were also interested in travel and trade. Some traders had traveled overland to Asia to purchase valuable items such as gold, silk, jewels, and spices. It was a long and dangerous journey, and some explorers began to think that they should try to find a sea route to Asia instead.

In Spain, an Italian named Christopher Columbus went to Queen Isabella and King Ferdinand for help. Not knowing of America, Columbus thought that he could find a fast and safe route to Asia and the Spice Islands by traveling west across the Atlantic Ocean. With Spain's money and support, Columbus set sail in 1492.

After five weeks at sea, Columbus's crew spotted land. They came ashore hap-

pily. They met the native people and celebrated a safe arrival. Columbus believed that he had reached the Spice Islands.

However, Columbus was wrong. He had not traveled nearly far enough to get to Asia. He had actually reached the Bahamas, just off the coast of North America.

Was Columbus's trip a failure? Not at all. Many people give Columbus the credit for opening the Americas to European exploration. His voyages led the way for many other explorers and settlers.

FINDING THE WAY AROUND

After Columbus, European explorers became obsessed with finding a sea route to Asia. In 1497, an Italian named John Cabot obtained support from England's king to do just that. On his journeys, he reached Newfoundland and explored the eastern coast of Canada.

In 1513, Vasco Núñez de Balboa led a Spanish expedition west across the ocean. When he reached Panama in Central America, he and his troops con-

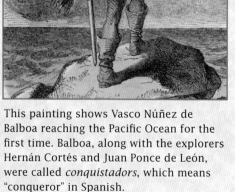

This painting shows Vasco Núñez de Balboa reaching the Pacific Ocean for the first time. Balboa, along with the explorers Hernán Cortés and Juan Ponce de León, were called *conquistadors*, which means "conqueror" in Spanish.

Ferdinand Magellan's crew gets the credit for being the first expedition to successfully travel around the world. They were the first to reach Tierra del Fuego, the southernmost tip of South America. They also brought along scientists to examine the new species of animals they found, including the penguin.

tinued traveling west over the land until they found the coastline of a new body of water. They were the first Europeans to see the Pacific Ocean from the west coast of the new continent.

In 1519, Ferdinand Magellan, a Portugese explorer, led an expedition of five ships across the Atlantic. His goal was to find a passage connecting the Atlantic and Pacific Oceans. Magellan died before the journey was over, but one of his ships accomplished an incredible feat: It became the first ship to circumnavigate, or travel all the way around, the globe.

French explorer Jacques Cartier also tried to find a passage to Asia. In 1535, he explored the St. Lawrence River and the southeastern part of Canada, near where the city of Montreal is today.

RICHES IN THE NEW WORLD

Explorers were unsuccessful in finding a short route across the sea from Europe to Asia. But they began to realize that the "New World" was full of valuable resources itself—furs to trade, fertile land, perhaps even gold and jewels. Soon explorers began traveling to North America on purpose, eager to take advantage of the riches they could find there.

Juan Ponce de León traveled from Spain to North America in 1513 and landed on the southern tip of Florida. He gets the credit for being the first European to set foot on land that is now the United States. According to legend, he

was searching for the Fountain of Youth, a mythical fountain whose waters would give eternal youth to anyone who drank from it.

Hernán Cortés was a Spaniard who explored Mexico in 1519. On his travels, he encountered the wealthy Aztec people. His armies overpowered the Aztecs, took control of Mexico, and claimed its gold and riches for Spain.

Henry Hudson, an English explorer who worked for the Dutch East India Company, sailed to North America in 1609. He explored what is now the Hudson River Valley, and his journeys led to the Dutch settlement of New Amsterdam on the island of Manhattan.

AMERICA'S FIRST CITY
St. Augustine, Florida, is the oldest city in the United States. It was founded in September 1565 by Spanish explorer Pedro Menéndez de Avilés. People have lived there ever since.

WELCOME TO NEW AMSTERDAM (I MEAN, NEW YORK!)
In 1626, Dutch explorer Peter Minuit traded some goods and supplies to the Manhatta people for the island of Manhattan. He named the settlement New Amsterdam. Then in 1664, King Charles II of England sent troops to take over the island. He renamed the city New York in honor of his brother, the Duke of York.

TRAVELING IN STYLE
The caravel was a kind of sailing ship invented in the 1400s. It was much smaller and lighter than other ships, which allowed it to move much more quickly. Because of its small size, it could travel upriver and in shallow waters as well as on the ocean. The caravel's sails were rigged differently than those on other ships so it could sail against the wind. Because of these new developments, the caravel was the perfect choice for explorers traveling long distances. In fact, two of the three ships on Columbus's first voyage—the *Niña* and the *Pinta*—were caravels.

SLAVERY IN THE COLONIES

Slavery has a long history in the United States. The first African slaves arrived in Jamestown in 1619. In the beginning, these people were indentured servants who began their lives in America in slavery but, after four to seven years of work, earned their freedom. Many poor European settlers who could not afford the ship's passage came to America in the same way. But after a time, African slaves lost the opportunity to work for their freedom. Why did slavery take hold so quickly in the colonies? Farms and plantations needed many cheap workers in order to be successful. Plantation owners realized that by using slave labor, they could make larger profits.

When Governor John White returned to the Roanoke Colony, he found two clues left by the missing Roanoke colonists. One was the word *CROATOAN* carved into the post of the fort, and *CRO* carved into a tree. Some people think that meant the colonists had moved to the island of Croatoan, but the truth of their disappearance remains unknown.

AMERICAN COLONIES

Once European countries realized that the land in North America was such a rich resource, they wanted to claim it for themselves. The best way to do that was to establish colonies: groups of people settling in the new land.

The colonies were good for the settlers as well as for their home countries in Europe. The settlers had the opportunity to make new lives in a new land. By farming or making products to trade, the colonists could grow rich. The home countries benefited by gaining more territory, more natural resources, and more wealth.

But there were risks, too. Early colonists had to rely on only themselves and the supplies that they brought with them. They worried about violent encounters with native people. There was no easy way to return to Europe if life became difficult. Even so, many colonists were ready for the adventure. It was a risk they were willing to take.

EARLY COLONISTS

England moved quickly to establish colonies in the Americas. In 1607, the first permanent English colonists arrived in Virginia. They called their settlement Jamestown, after King James I. Many of the settlers had agreed to come because they believed that they would find gold. It was a nasty surprise when they discovered no gold—only hard work.

Some years later, in 1620, the Pilgrims arrived in Plymouth, Massachusetts. The Pilgrims were actually two groups of people. One group was the Puritans (or Separatists), religious people who wanted to separate from the established religion and "purify" it. The other group consisted of people who were moving to the colonies for non-religious reasons. The Puritans called these people "Strangers."

The Separatists and the Strangers had some trouble getting along at first. So they signed an agreement called the Mayflower Compact. The Mayflower Compact set up a government and rules for all the colonists—Separatists and Strangers alike—to follow. It was an important document because it set the

THE MYSTERY OF ROANOKE

Twenty years before settlers came to Jamestown, English colonists settled on Roanoke Island, off the coast of North Carolina. Ships intending to return to Roanoke from England were delayed, and when they arrived a few years later with food and supplies, the settlers had disappeared. Their homes were deserted, and there was no sign of a struggle. What happened to the Lost Colony is a mystery to this day.

No one knows for sure on what day the first Thanksgiving took place because very little was written about it at the time. But we do know that the Pilgrims were very thankful for their success in the New World, so they hosted a feast for themselves and their American Indian friends to celebrate.

Old State House, Philadelphia, Pennsylvania

stage for the United States Constitution more than 150 years later.

It was hard for the Pilgrims to survive in their new land. They had a difficult time getting crops started, building homes, and hunting the new kinds of wildlife they found. Luckily, the nearby Wampanoag people gave advice, help, and supplies to the struggling settlers. Their first successful harvest was a time to celebrate, and the Pilgrims invited the Wampanoag people to share a three-day feast. This celebration has come to be known as the first Thanksgiving.

Settlers in the Massachusetts Bay Colony a bit further up the coast lived strict Puritan lives. People worked long hours on their farms. Everyone attended church, and they dressed, spoke, and behaved according to rules set by their church leaders. There were severe punishments for those who did not obey.

THIRTEEN COLONIES

The Pilgrims' hard work brought great success. And back in England, people took notice. Once the colonists who were in

Governors Palace, Williamsburg, Virginia

Jamestown and Massachusetts proved that it was possible to live successfully in America, more settlers were willing to make the journey across the Atlantic Ocean. Between 1607 and 1732, 13 British colonies were established along the east coast of America.

The New England colonies—Rhode Island, Massachusetts, Connecticut, and New Hampshire—were founded between 1623 and 1636. Many of the colonists who occupied them came to America to find religious or political freedom. They made their living through fishing and farming, and many of their corn and wheat crops were shipped to England for trade.

The Middle colonies—New York, New Jersey, Pennsylvania, and Delaware—were established between 1626 and 1682. While some colonists in Pennsylvania came for religious freedom, most people in the Middle Colonies came to get rich. The milder climate and rich soil of this region made it easier to grow crops there than in New England. In addition, many items, such as glass, leather, iron, and paper, were produced here.

The Southern colonies—Virginia, Maryland, North Carolina, South Carolina, and Georgia—were established between 1607 and 1732. The settlers in this area came primarily to make money. Farming was the main source of wealth in the Southern colonies: Large plantation owners grew crops such as tobacco, rice, and indigo.

WITCHES IN SALEM

Puritan life in Massachusetts was full of hard work and strict rules. But sometimes unusual things happened. In 1692, two Salem girls named Betty Parris and Abigail Williams claimed that an old slave named Tituba was a witch and that she had them under her control. During that year, Betty, Abigail, and their friends accused many people in the village of witchcraft. Many of them were sent to prison and put on trial. Some were killed—19 men and women were hanged, and one person was pressed to death. Finally, the accusations and the trials stopped. But it wasn't until 2001 that all of the accused witches were declared innocent. What motivated the girls to accuse so many people of witchcraft? We'll never know for sure.

OTHER SETTLEMENTS

The English colonies were not the only European settlements in North America. The Spanish were setting up missions in the southwest and along the west coast before English settlers founded Jamestown. One major goal of the missions was to spread Christianity to the native people there.

Meanwhile, the French had also established settlements across North America. They called their land in America "New France," and it stretched from the Quebec settlement of 1608 in the far north to Louisiana and all the way to the Gulf of Mexico in the south.

THE LAST COLONY

The last British colony in America was Georgia, which was founded in 1732. It was established for people in England who couldn't pay their debts: They could choose to go to prison, or they could go to Georgia instead.

A NEW NATION

The American Revolution brought about the birth of a new nation, but that nation's development was not always smooth.

Over the years, the colonies "grew up." Each colony created a working government. Farms produced healthy crops. Factories made valuable products that were shipped to England. But the colonists became unhappy with how Britain was treating them.

One main problem for the colonists was what they called "taxation without representation." The British government could decide what kinds of taxes the colonists had to pay, but the colonists could not vote for the leaders who made those decisions. They had no say in the decisions at all.

Sometimes it seemed the British government put taxes on everything: lead, glass, paper, paint, and even tea. The colonists protested by boycotting, or refusing to buy, British products. That didn't stop the taxes.

Next, in what was known as the Boston Tea Party, colonists dressed up as American Indians, sneaked onto ships in Boston Harbor, and dumped crates of tea overboard to protest taxes. But this didn't work, either.

The colonists realized they had to work together. In 1774, delegates, or representatives, from 12 of the 13 colonies (all but Georgia) met in Philadelphia at the First Continental Congress. They sent a letter to King George III in England asking for more control over their own government. Each colony also agreed to put together an army of minutemen, soldiers who could be ready at a moment's notice. The colonies realized that maybe it was time to break away from England altogether.

King George III

This map is similar to those printed during the first years of the country. Some of the states disagreed on how to divide the western territories, and different maps showed them belonging to different states. Finally the federal government took control of the territories.

REVOLUTION!

In May 1775, delegates—including Thomas Jefferson, Benjamin Franklin, John Adams, and George Washington—met at a Second Continental Congress. Some important

A MIDNIGHT RIDE

The first fighting of the Revolutionary War happened on April 19, 1775, in Lexington and Concord, Massachusetts. Patriot Paul Revere made a famous midnight horseback ride the previous night to warn the Americans that the British were coming.

This painting shows Benjamin Franklin, John Adams, and Thomas Jefferson working on the Declaration of Independence in Philadelphia. John Adams would later become America's second president, and Jefferson would become its third.

things happened at this meeting. One was that the delegates decided to form a Continental Army, with George Washington as the Commander in Chief.

Yet the delegates tried to make peace with England once more by sending the king the Olive Branch Petition, a letter asking him to address the colonists' complaints. But the king refused to receive it.

The delegates then decided to write up a document stating their ideas about forming a new country. Thomas Jefferson was in charge of writing this document, and it became the Declaration of Independence. The delegates voted to accept it on July 4, 1776.

Now the delegates realized the colonies could no longer ask the king for more rights or fair treatment. Instead, they decided to form their own country and fight for their independence.

WINNING THE WAR

Great Britain and the newly formed United States of America fought each other in the Revolutionary War from 1776 until 1781. The early days of the war were difficult for the Americans. The British army was well trained and well supplied. The Continental

George Washington crossing the Delaware River

THE FRENCH AND INDIAN WAR

About 20 years before the Revolutionary War, Britain and the American colonies fought a war against the French. The French had huge territories in North America, and the British wanted this land. So when the French built Fort Duquesne on the Ohio River in 1754, the British told them to leave. They didn't, and war broke out. The French had the Huron nation on their side and won many of the battles. England turned to the Iroquois nation for help. The Iroquois were enemies of the Huron and agreed to join the fight. By 1759, the British had won the war. In 1763, the French signed a treaty and gave up most of their land in North America.

General Cornwallis had 8,300 British troops with him when he arrived at Yorktown. But he was outnumbered by George Washington's army of over 17,000. Cornwallis surrendered after just a few weeks.

army had trouble organizing troops and didn't have the equipment the soldiers needed. A low point for the Americans was when troops suffered through the winter of 1777 in Valley Forge. One out of four soldiers died of sickness or starvation.

The tide turned when the French government sent troops and supplies, and when a German general named Baron von Steuben trained the American troops. Washington's army won important victories in Saratoga, Trenton, and Fort Vincennes. John Paul Jones led the American navy to many victories, as well.

Then the British troops headed south. They won battles in Savannah and Charleston, but the Continental army continued to put up a good fight. At Guilford Courthouse, General Cornwallis and the British army beat the Americans again. But this time Cornwallis's army was weakened: It had lost too many troops and supplies.

Cornwallis's soldiers limped on to Yorktown, Virginia, where American and French troops were able to surround them and besiege the city, refusing to let any supplies in or out. Cornwallis surrendered his troops on October 19, 1781. Though some fighting broke out after Yorktown, the Revolutionary War was over.

In 1783, England and the United States signed the Treaty of Paris. In this treaty, England recognized America's independence. The United States was finally free to govern itself.

BENEDICT ARNOLD

Benedict Arnold was an American general who became a spy for the British and plotted to let them capture the fort at West Point, New York. The plan was discovered, and Arnold escaped to England.

George Washington is the only American president to have been elected unanimously: He received every possible vote. His inauguration ceremony, the official celebration that started off his term in office, took place in New York City, which was America's capital in 1789.

A NEW KIND OF GOVERNMENT

The United States had a difficult challenge: how to create a working democracy, which is a government in which the citizens elect the leaders. America's first try was with the Articles of Confederation in 1781. This document set up a very weak federal, or national, government, so the states could have strong local governments. The federal government was allowed to raise an army, print money, and communicate with foreign countries. But it could not collect taxes or control trade. The Articles of Confederation also did not allow for a main leader, such as a king or a president.

The Articles of Confederation did not work well, so in 1787, delegates gathered at a Constitutional Convention in Philadelphia to write a new constitution. This document created a much stronger federal government with three parts: a legislative branch to make the laws, an executive branch to carry out the laws, and a judicial branch to

THE BILL OF RIGHTS

After the Constitution was finished, some Americans decided to make changes to it. Such changes are called *amendments*. James Madison wrote the first ten amendments to protect important personal freedoms, such as the freedom of speech and the freedom of religious worship. Madison's document is called the Bill of Rights. It was ratified, or approved, in 1791.

THE WAR OF 1812

The United States went to war with Britain one more time, in 1812. Britain and France were at war with each other in Europe, and Britain wanted America to join the war on its side. The United States tried to stay neutral, not taking sides at all, but the British began forcing American sailors to work for the British navy. In addition, the British refused to leave some of their American forts. For the next two years, American and British armies battled— the British even attacked Washington, D.C., and set fire to the White House! But the Americans defended themselves and proved they could protect their independence. The British and the Americans signed a peace treaty, the Treaty of Ghent, in 1814.

make sure that the laws are fair. The legislative branch is made up of Congress: the House of Representatives and the Senate. The executive branch is made up of the president and everyone who works for the president. The judicial branch is made up of the Supreme Court and the national court system.

The Constitution was ratified, or approved, in 1788. And in 1789, George Washington became the first president of the United States. The country was on its way.

A GROWING COUNTRY

Soon, the United States began looking beyond the borders of its 13 colonies. Some people supported the idea of Manifest Destiny: They believed the United

States should grow so that it stretched from the Atlantic Ocean to the Pacific Ocean. With that goal in mind, the government began taking and buying land.

Thomas Jefferson became president in 1801. One of the most important things he did during his presidency was to buy the Louisiana Purchase from France in 1803. It was a huge piece of land: It doubled the size of the United States!

Then Jefferson sent two explorers, Meriwether Lewis and William Clark, on an expedition to the Pacific Ocean. Their group of travelers was called the Corps of Discovery, and from 1804 to 1806 they mapped, drew, and wrote descriptions of what they found. Their detailed records helped Americans learn more about the strange and mysterious West.

PIONEERS

Some Americans were eager to go west and see for themselves. They wanted more land, more open spaces, and more opportunities to get rich.

Daniel Boone was a pioneer who explored many parts of the West. In the late 1700s, he marked out a new trail called the Wilderness Road that led from eastern

Virginia into Kentucky. In later years, many pioneers used this as their route to the West.

New kinds of transportation made the move west cheaper and easier than ever before. Corduroy roads were laid with logs, and they were easier to use than muddy dirt roads. Steamboats allowed for quick, easy river travel. Canals, such as the Erie Canal, were built to provide a faster and smoother way to transport people and supplies. After the 1830s, steam locomotives were the fastest way to travel.

The pioneers were not moving into empty territory: It was land where Native American peoples had lived for hundreds of years. Clashes between pioneers and American Indians became more frequent as native people saw their ancestral lands being fenced off and taken away. In 1830, Congress passed the Indian Removal Act. This act claimed to be a way for Native American nations to trade their land for lands that were further west, but it caused many unwilling peoples to lose their homes.

In 1838, President Martin Van Buren chose to enforce the new law in Georgia, where the Cherokee people had lived for generations. The U.S. army rounded up 17,000 Cherokee and forced them to travel nearly 1,000 miles to new lands in Oklahoma. Most walked or rode horseback. Because of the severe winter weather,

When Daniel Boone reached Kentucky, he built a fort and a village that he called Boonesborough. In later years, he moved further west to Missouri because he thought that Kentucky had become "too crowded."

Erie Canal

During the 1850s, thousands of people moved west to find gold in California. In 1850, California's population was only about 93,000. By 1860, that number had jumped to about 380,000 people!

disease, and starvation, 4,000 Cherokee died on this journey, which is now called "The Trail of Tears."

A DIVIDED NATION

Slavery had been an important part of the American economy since colonial times. By the early 1800s, slavery had died out in the North, but it remained important to Southern farmers, who felt that they needed slave labor on their tobacco and cotton plantations. Life for slaves in the South was very difficult, full of hard work and cruel treatment. Slaves had no control over where they lived, what they did, or even whom they married. They were bought and sold as property, and were often abused by their masters.

Abolitionists were people who believed that slavery should be abolished, or ended. They helped slaves escape to freedom along a secret route through the

Harriet Tubman was an escaped slave who risked her life to help other slaves escape north to freedom. In the years before the Civil War, she led nearly 300 slaves, including her own parents, along the dangerous Underground Railroad to the North.

South and the North and into Canada called the Underground Railroad. They also demanded national laws to make slavery illegal across the United States. By the 1850s, people all over America were talking about the slavery issue.

BREAKING AWAY

Most Southerners believed that each state should choose for itself whether or not to have slavery. They were afraid that the new president, Abraham Lincoln, would work against that idea. So in 1860, South Carolina seceded, or broke away, from the United States. Then six more states seceded: Mississippi, Florida, Alabama, Georgia, Louisiana, and Texas. They formed a new country, which they called the Confederate States of America.

President Lincoln realized that American troops would need to fight in order to bring the United States back together. In 1861, Confederate troops attacked U.S. soldiers at Fort Sumter in Charleston, South Carolina. The Union, or the North, was now at war with the Confederacy, or the South. Four more Southern states seceded to join the Confederacy: Arkansas, North Carolina, Virginia, and Tennessee. For the next four years, soldiers fought to determine if the United States could survive.

UNCLE TOM'S CABIN
In 1852, Harriet Beecher Stowe wrote a book called *Uncle Tom's Cabin*. It told the tragic story of a slave named Tom, and it pointed out the evils of slavery. This novel caused many people to believe that slavery should be abolished in the United States.

BROTHER AGAINST BROTHER

Many people have called the Civil War "the war of brother against brother." That's because Americans were fighting other Americans. Often, family members found themselves on different sides of the war because of where they lived or because they had different beliefs.

Each side in the conflict had advantages. The South had a strong general named Robert E. Lee, whose military skills inspired his troops. It also had well-trained soldiers who fought fiercely to protect their own lands, since most of the Civil War was fought in the Southern states.

The North had a larger population, which meant more soldiers for the army. Northern states also had more factories, so it was easier for them to keep their army supplied with food, gear, and weapons.

Soldiers fought in bloody battles at places such as Bull Run, Antietam, and Gettysburg. Over time, the North won more battles. The Northern general, Ulysses S. Grant, was determined to make the South surrender. By 1865, the Confederate army was weak, sick, and exhausted. Lee surrendered his troops in April 1865, at Appomattox Court House, Virginia.

A NEW AMERICA

Abraham Lincoln did not want to punish the South for leaving the Union. Instead, he asked for a "gentle peace" so that the country could come back together. Sadly, Lincoln did not see his dream come true. A Southerner named John Wilkes Booth shot and killed him just days after the war ended.

The time period after the Civil War when the South rebuilt itself is called Reconstruction. For many, it was a hopeful time of change. Congress ratified amendments to the Con-

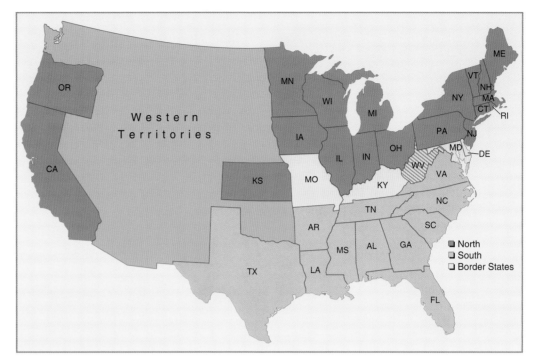

The Union and the Confederacy, with border states (not officially supporting either side) in yellow. West Virginia started the war in the Confederacy as part of Virginia but broke away from that state and joined the Union in 1863. The Western Territories also belonged to the Union.

THE BLOODIEST BATTLE

Gettysburg is one of the best-known battles of the Civil War. From July 1 to July 3, 1863, Union and Confederate soldiers fought in humid summer weather in Gettysburg, Pennsylvania. By the time the battle had ended, more than 51,000 soldiers had been killed or wounded. Historians believe this battle was the turning point in the war, because it stopped the Confederate army, led by Robert E. Lee, from moving north. Four months later, President Lincoln would visit this battleground and give his most famous speech, the Gettysburg Address.

stitution that abolished slavery and gave all men the right to vote. African-Americans were elected to Congress and had a voice in the government for the first time. A government organization called the Freedmen's Bureau helped freed slaves find homes and jobs.

Unfortunately, Reconstruction was not successful. President Andrew Johnson, a Southerner who did not support Reconstruction, interfered with Congress's plans. Southern states also found other ways to deny African-Americans their rights. They charged a poll tax that people had to pay in order to vote. They also passed laws to segregate, or separate, people based on their race. African-Americans would have to fight for many more years to get equal treatment in jobs, in schools, and in the government.

GROWTH AND CHANGE

The country reunited after the Civil War, and industry and inventions changed life in the United States.

If you had been born in the 19th century, you would have seen an incredible change in American life from 1850 to 1900. Inventors created new tools and machines. Factories developed ways to produce goods quickly and cheaply. America was becoming a wealthy, powerful nation.

A CHANGING WORLD

The Industrial Revolution began in England in the late 1770s. Factories changed the way they did business. Instead of having one person make a product from start to finish, the process was divided up into many smaller jobs. Each worker performed just one job over and over again to make part of a product many times. For instance, if a worker put a back wheel on a cart, that person would put the back wheel on cart after cart after cart. This process was called the *division of labor*. One example of this is the assembly line. What was the benefit?

Each product was finished more quickly, and the factory owners made larger profits.

Some factory owners in America took the lessons learned in England and applied

The development of assembly lines and factories led to new jobs. The work at textile mills like this one was often boring, and the pay was low. But these jobs gave many women the opportunity to work outside the home for the first time.

This painting shows Alexander Graham Bell's first public demonstration of the telephone in 1876. People were amazed to hear a live voice come out of a series of wires.

Orville and Wilbur Wrights' airplane was called a biplane because it had two sets of wings on either side of the body. Biplanes were the most common type of aircraft until the 1930s, when monoplanes—planes with only one set of wings—came on the scene.

them to their own businesses. In Massachusetts, people built textile mills to produce cloth. By breaking the job down into many small tasks, mill owners made huge profits. Other kinds of factories followed soon after in all parts of the country.

NEW TIMES, NEW INVENTIONS

New inventions also changed life forever. For hundreds of years, it had been difficult to communicate with people over long distances. But in 1837, Samuel Morse sent the first telegraph message. A telegraph is a machine that sends messages by using electrical signals that translate into an alphabetic code of dots and dashes. By 1866, people could send telegraph messages across the Atlantic Ocean. In 1876, Alexander Graham Bell used telegraph technology to invent a machine that could transmit the human voice over long distances. It was called the telephone.

Transportation also changed. At the end of the 19th century, many different inventors developed a kind of "horseless carriage," also known as an automobile or a car. An American named Henry Ford invented a special kind of automobile. His car had interchangeable parts, which meant that the parts of one could easily be put together, removed, or replaced with

those of another. That made his automobile easier to make and cheaper to buy than anyone else's.

Americans were also looking for a way to fly. In 1903, brothers Orville and Wilbur Wright invented an airplane that they flew successfully over the beach in Kitty Hawk, North Carolina.

One of the most famous inventors of the 1800s was Thomas Edison. He created one incredible invention after another: the phonograph (an early version of the record player), the movie camera, and even the electric lightbulb!

THE MODEL T
Henry Ford's first big-selling car was the Model T. Introduced in 1908, at one point new Model Ts sold for as little as $260, an affordable price for most families. In some years, it came only in black— the fastest-drying paint Ford could find!

John D. Rockefeller

Cornelius Vanderbilt

Andrew Carnegie

BIG BUSINESS

Meanwhile, other Americans took advantage of all the new technology by applying it to industry. They built successful factories and companies, and the business owners, called industrialists, became incredibly rich.

John D. Rockefeller was in the oil business. His company, Standard Oil, became the largest company in the world. Andrew Carnegie founded the Carnegie Steel Company, which later became U.S. Steel. Cornelius Vanderbilt made his money building railroads, and J. P. Morgan made his fortune in international banking. Morgan had so much money that he was able to help out the American government during a depression in 1895 by loaning the government $62 million.

Some of these businesses became so big and so powerful that they were able to control the way other companies operated. Sometimes they put those other companies out of business. The successful businesses became monopolies. That means they had no competition and they could charge any prices they wanted for their products. Some companies also formed trusts. The members of a trust agreed to charge a particular price for a product so they would not have to worry about competition. In this way, they were like monopolies.

Industrialists such as Rockefeller and Morgan became famous around the world for their huge bank accounts and their incredible lifestyles. However, many of them also became philanthropists. That means they donated a lot of their money to help other people by funding libraries, hospitals, and schools.

IMMIGRATION

As the United States became wealthier and more powerful, people in other countries took notice. They, too, wanted the opportunities that could be found in America: political freedom, religious freedom, and the freedom to make better lives for themselves and their families.

THE STATUE OF LIBERTY

The Statue of Liberty stands in New York Harbor. For many immigrants, it was a symbol of freedom and opportunity. The statue was dedicated in 1886 as a gift to America from France.

Immigrant families crowded into tenements in bustling neighborhoods such as this one. Families had such limited indoor space that a lot of living took place outdoors—from hanging laundry to sleeping on fire escapes, even to playing a game of stickball on the street.

From 1850 to 1900, millions of immigrants came to America from all over the world. There was plenty of room for them, too: America needed more people to work in factories and to settle the West.

Over the years, different groups of immigrants made their way to America. Thousands of Irish immigrants came in the 1840s and 1850s because potato crops were failing in Ireland and people were starving. In the 1850s, Chinese immigrants came in order to work building the railroads. Throughout the 1860s and 1870s, immigrants came from western European countries such as England, Scotland, Denmark, and France. By the 1880s and 1890s, most immigrants to America were from European countries that were further east, such as Germany, Italy, Poland, Russia, and Greece.

Most immigrants traveled by boat and came through New York City. They passed through Ellis Island, an island in New York Harbor that was set up to examine passengers to make sure they were healthy and ready to work. Some immigrants with contagious diseases had to stay at Ellis Island until they were well. Immigrants who failed the tests were sent back to their home countries.

THE GREAT MIGRATION

In the 1890s, life was still hard for African-Americans in the South. "Jim Crow" laws (named for a black character in a popular song) kept black and white people apart. This was called *segregation*. African-Americans didn't have access to the same schools, neighborhoods, restaurants, and stores that white people did. For that reason, many African-Americans decided to leave the South. They moved north and west in order to escape segregation and discrimination. They hoped to find opportunities in the big cities of the West, and they settled in places such as Kansas City, St. Louis, and Chicago. This movement has been called the Great Migration.

Many immigrants chose to live in urban areas, or cities. It was easier to find work in a city because of the number of factories. Immigrants also chose big cities because they could find other immigrants who shared their language and culture. In New York City, for example, different neighborhoods sprang up where people from the same home country set up shops, restaurants, and other businesses that reminded them of home. You can visit places such as Chinatown and Little Italy in New York City to this day.

It wasn't easy to be an immigrant in the city. Families were crowded together in tiny apartments in buildings called tenements, often without heat or running water. People worked for long hours and little pay in small factories called sweatshops.

MOVING WEST

Some immigrants chose to leave the cities behind and move west. In 1848, people discovered gold in California. As a result, many immigrants headed straight to the gold mines, hoping to become instant millionaires.

Another thing that drew a number of immigrants west was the Homestead Act, which Congress passed in 1862. This law allowed settlers to buy 160 acres in the West for a small fee. If they could work the land successfully for five years, they could keep it.

How did people travel west? Many made the journey in groups of wagons called wagon trains, traveling in covered wagons pulled by horses or oxen. It was a

Native Americans knew that the Transcontinental Railroad would mean the end of their way of life. So many American Indians of the Plains tore up railroad tracks and attacked railroad workers and train cars.

slow and dangerous journey. Many more people were willing to make the trip west once the Transcontinental Railroad was finished in 1869. This railroad connected the east and west coasts of the United States. It made cross-country travel cheaper, easier, and faster.

The flood of settlers made life more difficult for Native American people living in the West. Indian nations such as the Blackfoot and the Sioux fought to protect their land from newcomers who wanted to fence it in and claim it. The American government sent troops to protect the settlers, and there were many violent conflicts. In 1876, General George Custer and 600 American troops battled 2,000 members of the Cheyenne, Lakota, and Arapaho nations after the Native Americans refused to leave their lands in South Dakota. The Native Americans won the battle, killing Custer and many of his soldiers.

THE REFORMERS

While some Americans found wealth and success, others struggled to survive. Many spent long hours in factories, working for little pay in unsafe conditions. Immigrants suffered in dirty, crowded tenements. Poor fami-

lies didn't have access to clean water or good schools. Many poor children had to work, so they couldn't go to school. There were no rules in place to protect the people who needed the most help.

Some Americans decided to speak out against these conditions. They were called *reformers,* and they worked for change. Some were journalists. Some were leaders and organizers. All of them cared about helping others.

SPEAKING OUT

Muck is another name for dirt. And a *muckraker* is someone who digs up the dirt. Beginning in the late 1800s, a group of journalists wrote articles about business cheats and unfair situations. The journalists were called muckrakers because they "dug up the dirt" on rich, powerful people who took advantage of others. Ida Tarbell wrote articles about Rockefeller's company, Standard Oil, and the unfair strategies it used to put other oil companies out of business. Caricatures by cartoonist Thomas Nast showed how some New York politicians broke the law by paying people to vote for them. Upton Sinclair wrote a novel called *The Jungle* about the poor conditions in meat-packing factories.

Other reformers made their marks as leaders and organizers. Samuel Gompers was a labor leader: He brought workers

In May 1886, thousands of workers organized a strike and marched in Chicago to show their support for an eight-hour workday. The marches turned into riots when local police attacked strikers. Eleven people died, and many were wounded in what came to be known as the Haymarket Riot.

GEORGE WASHINGTON CARVER

Born a slave around 1864, a man named George Washington Carver worked hard to get an education and make a good life for himself. By 1896, Carver was a valued scientist and teacher working at Booker T. Washington's Tuskegee Institute. Today, Carver is best known for his work with peanuts. His experiments led him to come up with almost 300 different uses for the peanut, including peanut butter, Worcestershire sauce, linoleum, instant coffee, and glue. So next time you make yourself a peanut-butter-and-jelly sandwich, you can thank Dr. Carver!

ton founded the Tuskegee Institute, a school that trained African-Americans as carpenters, teachers, and printers. He believed that African-Americans needed to work for economic equality by going to school and getting good jobs. W.E.B. DuBois was an African-American reformer who felt differently. He believed that political equality was more important than economic equality, and with others he founded the National Association for the Advancement of Colored People (NAACP) to fight discrimination.

A PRESIDENT TAKES A STAND

President Theodore "Teddy" Roosevelt was a reformer, too. When he became president in 1901, he decided he needed to make big businesses operate more responsibly. He believed that trusts and monopolies were not fair, because they forced other companies out of business and made customers pay the prices set by the monopolies. So Roosevelt enforced the Sherman Anti-Trust Act, which limited trusts. Over the years, he broke up many trusts and monopolies.

Roosevelt was also outraged by the irresponsible ways that factories produced food products. He discovered that many companies made and sold food that was rotten, unhealthy, and dangerous to eat. So he supported laws such as the Pure Food and Drug Act and the Meat Inspection Act to make sure that food was safe for all.

Roosevelt also cared about the environment and believed in conservation, or saving natural spaces. He worried that America's open land was disappearing as the population rose and cities grew. Roosevelt worked with a naturalist named John Muir to set up national parks and nature reserves across the United States.

No one expected Theodore Roosevelt to become president! In the 1900 presidential election, William McKinley was elected president, with Teddy Roosevelt as his vice-president. Roosevelt took over as president after McKinley was assassinated in 1901. He is the youngest man ever to achieve that office.

together to demand more pay and better working conditions. Mother Jones was another labor leader who focused on helping working children. She organized children's marches and demanded that children work fewer hours so that they would have more time to go to school.

Reformers also cared about helping immigrants. Jacob Riis was a journalist who took many photographs of immigrant life in the poor neighborhoods of the Lower East Side in New York City. He wrote a book called *How the Other Half Lives,* and its photographs helped Americans see for the first time just how difficult life was for many families. In Chicago, Jane Addams founded Hull House, a settlement house where immigrants could learn English, get job training and child care, and receive health care.

Some reformers worked for the rights of African-Americans. Booker T. Washing-

THE PRESIDENT AND THE TEDDY BEAR

Teddy Roosevelt loved hunting. But on one trip, he came across a bear that was injured and refused to shoot it. A toymaker in New York heard this story and renamed his stuffed bears "Teddy's bears" in Roosevelt's honor. The word "teddy bear" is still with us today.

AMERICA IN THE WORLD

Following the turn of the century, the United States became bolder in involving itself in international affairs.

★ ★ ★

At the end of World War I, President Woodrow Wilson proposed a peace plan. One part of his plan was for the countries of the world to form an organization to help solve world conflicts. This led to the League of Nations and later to the United Nations.

The 20th century brought even more changes to America. Society evolved as even more new technology came on the scene. Americans also faced serious challenges, including an economic depression and two world wars.

THE WORLD AT WAR

As the 1900s began, Europe was a tense place. The German government wanted to expand its boundaries and take over land that it believed belonged to Germany. Other European countries had signed treaties, or agreements, to defend each other in case Germany invaded. In 1914, an Austrian archduke named Franz Ferdinand was assassinated, and his death caused several countries to declare war on each other.

That was how World War I began. Germany, Austria, and the Ottoman Empire (which included modern-day Turkey and more) came together as the Central Powers. They battled the Allies, a group of countries that included Russia, Great Britain, and France. Though many believed that the war would be over in a matter of months, it soon became clear that this would be much worse. It came to be called "the war to end all wars," and it was the deadliest war in history to that point.

Why was World War I so deadly? New technology made killing easier than ever

ARMISTICE DAY

Armistice means "truce" or "peace." Armistice Day is the day that World War I ended. It is celebrated around the world on November 11 at 11:00 A.M.—the 11th hour on the 11th day of the 11th month.

WOMEN'S SUFFRAGE

In the early part of the 20th century, American women were working hard to gain suffrage, or the right to vote. They argued that they should have the right to choose their leaders, just as American men did. The women's suffrage movement had begun back in 1848, when Elizabeth Cady Stanton organized an important meeting in Seneca Falls, New York. Since then, women such as Susan B. Anthony, Lucy Stone, and Amelia Bloomer had joined the fight. Their hard work paid off: In 1920, Congress passed the 19th Amendment, which gave women the right to vote. Even so, it would still be many more years before women achieved equal access to education, jobs, and other opportunities.

before. Airplanes battled in the sky. Submarines sank unsuspecting ships. Tanks, machine guns, and bombs made combat quick and impersonal. Poisonous gas choked, blinded, and killed soldiers on the battlefield.

AMERICA JOINS THE FIGHT

At first, the United States was not involved in World War I. Following the Monroe Doctrine, the United States tried to remain isolationist—it chose not to be involved in other countries' problems or conflicts. However, many Americans argued that the nation should get involved and support the Allies. It became harder for Americans to ignore what was happening overseas. In 1915, the Germans sunk the *Lusitania,* a British ocean liner. More than 100 of the passengers who died were Americans.

In 1917, President Woodrow Wilson called for war on the Central Powers. He believed that the United States needed to "make the world safe for democracy." American troops and supplies were just what the Allies needed. They won the war by November 1918.

THE ROARING TWENTIES

After the end of World War I, a period of prosperity—wealth and success—began in America. Nothing like it had ever been seen before. The 1920s are often called "The Roaring Twenties" because of the excitement and energy that people felt during this time.

Companies were growing, selling more products, and making bigger profits. People could benefit from this growth by investing money in the stock market. Companies sold shares of stock, which allowed partial ownership of the company. By buying stock in a company, people could make money every time the company did. The stock market grew. Everyone seemed to be profiting. Many people felt rich.

With all that extra money, Americans could afford to buy new things—and lots of them. They bought new cars, new radios, and new clothes. They spent money on new kinds of entertainment, such as movies and records.

New art and music also appeared on the scene. In New York City, the African-American neighborhood of Harlem had a rebirth of music, art, and culture. It was called the Harlem Renaissance. Jazz musicians such as Duke Ellington performed, while writers such as Zora Neale Hurston and artists such as Romare Bearden created amazing works.

In 1919, Congress passed the Prohibition amendment, which made the sale of alcohol illegal. This law was intended to make people behave more responsibly, but instead it backfired. For many, drinking alcohol became a secretive and glamorous activity. Secret clubs called speakeasies sprang up where people could drink alcohol and listen to jazz. Prohibition lasted until 1933, when another Constitutional amendment canceled it.

The 1920s became all about having a good time and enjoying prosperity. But it wouldn't be long before that fun would spin out of control.

CRASH!

The Roaring Twenties ended with a crash. On "Black Tuesday," October 29, 1929, the stock market "crashed," which means that the value of stocks dropped by a huge amount. Millions of people had invested their life savings in the stock market, and as a result many people lost everything. The Great Depression had begun.

What had happened? During the 1920s, people believed that the value of stocks would rise forever, and some people got greedy. They began investing in the stock market in risky and illegal ways.

During the Roaring Twenties, women cut their hair into short styles called "bobs" and tried out daring new fashions, including dresses that showed their knees and shoulders. These women were nicknamed "flappers."

CHARLES LINDBERGH
One of the most famous people of the 1920s was pilot Charles Lindbergh. In 1927, Lindbergh became the first person to fly across the Atlantic Ocean by himself. He flew from Long Island, New York, to Paris, France, in $33\frac{1}{2}$ hours.

Some people borrowed money from banks to buy stocks. When the market crashed, they couldn't repay their loans. With so many people unable to repay, many banks themselves had to close.

THE GREAT DEPRESSION

The stock market crash began a domino effect. As banks closed, factories and businesses closed, too. At the height of the Depression, one out of every four people was out of work. Without jobs, people couldn't pay their rents or mortgages, and many families became homeless. Some set up shanty-towns, which were groups of shacks made from cardboard or tin. They were nicknamed "Hoover-villes" as an insult to President Herbert Hoover, because many people believed he was doing nothing to end the Depression.

America's problems were made even worse by a terrible drought that ruined crops across the Midwest. Without rain, windstorms blew away topsoil and ruined farms, and Oklahoma, Texas, and Arkansas became known as the "Dust Bowl."

During the Depression, many people across the country depended on help from others for food and shelter. Some people waited in long lines for free meals in places called soup kitchens.

A NEW DEAL

Hope was around the corner. Franklin Delano Roosevelt was elected president in 1932, and his mission was to lead America out of the Depression.

Roosevelt took a practical approach to solving America's problems. He offered the country a "New Deal," which was a series of programs to get Americans working again. The Civilian Conservation Corps sent workers into national parks to build trails, manage forests, and construct buildings. The

Works Progress Administration created all kinds of new jobs, from painting murals on public buildings to sending writers to the South to interview former slaves.

The New Deal also included laws to protect sick people, children, and the elderly. The Social Security Act set up a "safety net" to provide money, food, and health care to these needy people.

Americans were working again, and the nation was finally getting back on its feet.

PROBLEMS IN EUROPE AND ASIA

America wasn't the only place suffering in the 1930s. Countries around the world were also struggling through a depression. In many cases, these countries elected strong leaders, dictators who promised to solve the economic problems but soon took complete control over the governments.

Italy elected Benito Mussolini. Russia and neighboring countries, which together were known as the Soviet Union, chose Joseph Stalin. In Japan, the military controlled the government. The Japanese wanted to take more land for their country, so they invaded Manchuria, parts of China, and French Indochina, which included modern-day Laos, Vietnam, and Cambodia.

In Germany, Adolf Hitler's Nazi Party made deals with other political parties, and Hitler was named chancellor in 1933. Like the other dictators, he promised to solve Germany's problems by making Germany strong again. Unfortunately, he did that by scapegoating, or blaming, part of the German community: its Jews. Hitler created a systematic plan to wipe out all Jewish people in Europe.

Like Japan, Germany also began taking land. In 1938 and 1939, Germany took over Austria and Czechoslovakia. Other European countries were worried, but they were willing to compromise with Hitler in the hopes of avoiding war. Then Hitler invaded Poland in 1939. France and Britain decided that he had to be stopped. They declared war on Germany. World War II had begun.

AMERICA GETS INVOLVED

Once again, many Americans believed that the United States should stay out of the war in Europe and Asia. But others thought that it was America's responsibility to get involved.

On December 7, 1941, Japanese planes attacked American ships and planes in Pearl Harbor, Hawaii. More than 2,000 Americans died. The next day, the United States declared war on Japan. A few days later, the United States was also at war with Germany.

By 1942, much of the world was involved in the conflict. The Axis powers included Germany, Italy, and Japan. The Allies included Britain, the United States, the Soviet Union, and a French army led by General Charles de Gaulle.

THE HOLOCAUST

Hitler's attempt to kill the Jews and other minorities of Europe is known as the Holocaust. He and members of his Nazi party built concentration camps across Europe. At camps such as Auschwitz, Bergen-Belsen, and Treblinka, victims were separated from their families, forced to work, starved, and murdered. From the early 1930s until the camps were liberated by Allied troops in 1945, more than six million Jews died, along with millions of other victims such

as Poles, Serbs, Gypsies (Roma and Sinti), homosexuals, and disabled people. Today, museums such as the United States Holocaust Memorial Museum in Washington, D.C., and the Museum of Tolerance in Los Angeles, California, tell the story of the Holocaust in the hopes that such an awful event will never happen again.

President Franklin Roosevelt (*center*) meets with British Prime Minister Winston Churchill (*left*) and Soviet Premier Joseph Stalin (*right*) to make plans for World War II.

The United States sprang into action. Troops traveled overseas to Europe and Asia. On the home front, Americans helped the war effort by rationing, or limiting, the supplies they used so the rest could go to the soldiers. People also recycled anything that could be used to produce war goods, such as metal, rubber, oil, and glass.

In order to help the war effort, many women took jobs outside of their homes for the first time. During the course of the war, the number of American women working outside the home rose from 12 to 18 million.

By some estimates, the atomic bombs that destroyed Hiroshima and Nagasaki killed close to 110,000 Japanese citizens and injured around 130,000 more.

The home front's biggest contribution to the war effort was in production. Factories operated around the clock to make tanks, airplanes, guns, and ammunition. With many men at war, women left their homes and went to work in the factories.

Over years of fighting, the Allied forces gradually gained strength and won many battles against the Axis. June 6, 1944, was a turning point in the war: Known as "D-Day," it was the day Allied troops landed on the beaches of Normandy, France. More than 154,000 Allied troops fought that day, arriving by boat or by parachute to take back the European continent from Nazi Germany. With this important victory, it was only a matter of time until Allied troops made it to Berlin and forced Germany to surrender.

The war against Japan was also a long, hard fight. Allied troops battled the Japanese army and navy on many islands in the Pacific, in hot weather and difficult conditions. The Japanese fought fiercely. They did not surrender until August 1945, after the United States dropped atomic bombs on the Japanese cities of Hiroshima and Nagasaki.

FDR AND HARRY TRUMAN

Harry S. Truman was Roosevelt's vice president during his last term. Roosevelt died in April 1945, shortly before the end of the war. It was Truman who had to make the difficult decision of whether to use the atomic bomb to end the war with Japan.

Part of D-Day's success was due to the fact that the Allies successfully tricked the Axis into thinking that the attack would take place farther north, in Norway, and farther south, near the French town of Calais.

MODERN TIMES

A superpower after World War II, the United States faced changes in the world and at home.

After winning World War II, armies from the United States, Great Britain, France, and the Soviet Union occupied the nations they had defeated. Allied leaders were responsible for rebuilding countries and governments across Europe and Asia. Life also changed within the United States.

A WORLD POWER AND A COLD WAR

One of the first things the Allies did in 1945 was establish the United Nations, an organization made up of countries from around the world. The goal of the United Nations was to help countries resolve conflicts peacefully and to avoid war.

This was not an easy task. Though the Soviet Union had sided with the Allies during World War II, its communist government was very different from the democratic governments of the United States, Great Britain, and France. The Soviet Union refused to remove troops from many Eastern European countries, including the eastern half of Germany. Stalin was determined to rule these countries: He did not allow free elections, he controlled newspapers and radio broadcasts, and he cut off communication with the West. Winston Churchill, the Prime Minister of Great Britain during World War II, said that an "Iron Curtain" had fallen over Eastern Europe.

The Soviet government wanted to control Eastern Europe and spread communism. The United States, along with Great Britain and France, wanted to preserve democratic governments. These conflicting views caused the Cold War between the Soviet Union and its former Allies. It was called a "cold" war because there was never any direct fighting, though relations between the countries were not good. People worried that the Cold War would become a "hot" war, involving actual fighting. By this time, both the Soviet Union and the United States had developed nuclear weapons, so any kind of conflict could be extremely destructive.

In 1949, the United States, France, Great Britain, and other countries created an alliance to protect each other in case of a Soviet attack. They called their alliance the North Atlantic Treaty Organization, or NATO.

From the original 12 nations that signed the 1949 North Atlantic Treaty, NATO has expanded to 26 member countries in Europe and North America.

When the United Nations was founded in 1945, it included 51 countries. Today, 191 nations belong to this organization. Although the UN buildings are in New York City, they are considered to be international territory.

WITCH HUNTS

In the early 1950s, Senator Joseph McCarthy took advantage of Americans' fear of communism. He accused many innocent Americans of being communists and spies for the Soviet Union, and he

What Is Communism?

Communists believe that a perfect society is one where all citizens share the wealth equally. In a communist country, the government owns the major industries and businesses, such as farms, factories, and mines, and the profits are shared equally by all the people. During the second half of the 20th century, the Soviet Union and China both had large, powerful communist governments. Democratic countries such as the United States and Great Britain thought communism was harmful because the governments did not allow individual people to own businesses or make free choices about their lives. Soviet Russia and China also denied individuals many freedoms, such as the right to vote for their leaders and the right to speak their minds openly in public.

cratic country of South Korea in 1950, American troops entered the conflict on the side of the South Koreans. Their goal was to drive the North Koreans out.

Then China, which also had a communist government, entered the war on the North Korean side. President Truman worried that with two large countries involved, the war could escalate and become a worldwide conflict. President Truman began the peace process, and President Dwight D. Eisenhower continued it. By 1953, the Korean War had ended without endangering other countries.

THE VIETNAM WAR

A similar conflict developed in the Asian country of Vietnam. By the late 1950s, the country had split in two. North Vietnam had a communist government, and South Vietnam had a democratic government. In the early 1960s, Presidents John F. Kennedy and Lyndon Johnson sent American advisers to help the South Vietnamese. Still, the conflict grew larger. Then in 1964, Johnson sent thousands of troops.

The American choice to get involved in Vietnam was based on the "domino theory." Some people argued that if one country adopted a communist government, then other countries near it would follow. Some people believed that America could prevent the spread of communism throughout Asia by defending democracy in Vietnam. As time went on, the war in Vietnam became more complicated. Americans spoke out on both sides of the issue.

brought these people to talk to Congress. McCarthy accused people from all walks of life, from movie stars to army generals. As accused communists, many of these people found their lives were ruined: They lost jobs, homes, and the respect of their communities. Eventually, the government denounced Senator McCarthy for his actions. Today, McCarthy's hearings are also known as the communist "witch hunts."

THE KOREAN WAR

Throughout the 1950s and 1960s, the U.S. government was concerned about the spread of communism around the world. When the communist country of North Korea invaded the demo-

American soldiers found combat in Vietnam difficult. Enemy soldiers called the Viet Cong used guerilla tactics, hiding among trees and grasses to ambush American troops in surprise attacks.

CHANGES IN AMERICA

During the 1950s and 1960s, American society changed dramatically, as different groups of Americans fought for equal treatment. They wanted to make sure the rights in the Declaration of Independence and the Constitution and the promise of the American Dream applied to everyone.

THE CIVIL RIGHTS MOVEMENT

Since the end of the Civil War in 1865, segregation—the policy of separating people based on race—had been an established system in the South. And though most Northern cities weren't strictly segregated, racism—judging people based on their race—was common everywhere. African-Americans wanted civil rights: fair treatment and equal opportunities.

Things began to change in the 1950s. Groups of people, both black and white, came together to fight for civil rights. In 1954, the Supreme Court decided an important case called *Brown v. Board of Education.* In this case, lawyers argued that an African-American girl named Linda Brown should be able to go to the white school only seven blocks from her house

THE SPACE RACE

American science and technology also advanced during the 1950s and 1960s. The world was shocked when the Soviet Union launched the first satellite into space in 1957, and the United States began developing a space program to keep up with the Soviets. This was the beginning of the "space race"—a competition between the Soviet Union and the United States to explore outer space and land people on the moon. The American space program made rapid progress. In 1961, Alan Shepard became the first American to go into space. In 1962, John Glenn became the first American to orbit the Earth. And on July 16, 1969, Neil Armstrong, Edwin "Buzz" Aldrin, and Michael Collins made the first successful trip to the moon.

instead of having to travel to the black school 21 blocks away. When the Supreme Court agreed with Brown's lawyers, they also decided that segregation in any school in America was illegal. This was a huge step forward in making civil rights a reality.

Then in 1955, in Montgomery, Alabama, an African-American woman named Rosa Parks refused to give her seat on the bus to a white person. Her arrest led to a boycott of the bus system in Montgomery. That means civil rights workers refused to ride the buses until the city changed its rules about segregation.

Dr. Martin Luther King, Jr., was a pastor in Montgomery who helped organize the bus boycott and later became a leader of the civil rights movement. His

ASSASSINATIONS
The 1960s were dramatic years filled with strong leaders. Sadly, many of these leaders were assassinated, or killed, by others who did not agree with their views. President John F. Kennedy, Malcolm X, Senator Robert F. Kennedy, and Dr. Martin Luther King, Jr., were all assassinated.

On August 28, 1963, hundreds of thousands of Americans took part in a march on Washington, D.C., in order to speak out in favor of civil rights. Marchers gathered at the Lincoln Memorial to hear Dr. Martin Luther King, Jr., deliver his famous "I Have a Dream" speech.

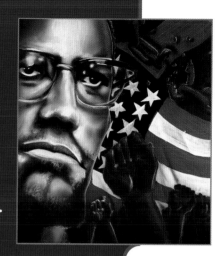

MALCOLM X

Not all civil rights leaders believed in nonviolence. Malcolm X led a group called the Nation of Islam. At first he believed that African-Americans should use violence to achieve their goals. But later in his life he came to agree with Dr. King's point of view.

goal was to ensure civil rights for everyone, regardless of race. Dr. King, a very inspirational speaker, believed that the civil rights movement should be nonviolent, so civil rights workers used peaceful strategies to make their voices heard. They marched. They organized boycotts. They held sit-ins, which means that they sat down in public places where they weren't normally allowed, such as at lunch counters, in order to draw attention to the issue of segregation.

In 1964, President Johnson signed the Civil Rights Act, which made segregation in public places illegal, and in 1965, he signed the Voting Rights Act, which protected the rights of African-Americans to vote. Both laws were important victories in the civil rights movement.

LA CAUSA

During the 1950s and 1960s, farm workers also fought for fair treatment. Migrant workers traveled from farm to farm, picking crops and working the land. They had difficult lives, often working for low wages in dangerous conditions. In 1962, César Chávez and Dolores Huerta established what would become United Farm Workers, an organization that worked for fair treatment. This movement was also called *La Causa,* which is Spanish for "the cause."

RIGHTS FOR WOMEN

For many American women during World War II, working in factories was their first experience with working outside their homes and making their own decisions. When the war ended and the men who fought in it returned home, many women were unwilling to give up their independence. By the 1960s, women were changing the rules about what they could do and

Supporters of women's rights took to the streets to support their cause in the 1960s and 1970s. They wanted to achieve an equal place with men in American society. In the center wearing a hat is Bella Abzug, a feminist leader who served in the U.S. House of Representatives.

César Chávez worked closely with farm workers to help them get fair treatment and better pay. He encouraged Americans to boycott, or stop buying, table grapes for five years, until the farm owners agreed to the farm workers' demands for better working conditions.

who they could be. They went to professional schools and took jobs as doctors, lawyers, and politicians. They fought to ensure their equal treatment in the workplace. Groups such as the National Organization for Women (NOW) worked for equal opportunities and equal pay. In the 1970s, some people tried to add a new amendment to the Constitution called the Equal Rights Amendment. It would make equal treatment of men and women the law of the land. This amendment has not yet been ratified, or accepted, by enough states to become law.

A NEW AMERICA

New technology and a shifting international scene changed everyday life in the United States again.

★ ★ ★

The 1960s and 1970s were a period of unrest in America. Many Americans were unhappy with what the government was doing at home and around the world, and they wanted to do something about it. Students in particular wanted to make their voices heard, and they spoke out on a number of issues. High school and college campuses were the sites of marches, protests, and sit-ins.

The war in Vietnam was a focus for many protesters. As more American soldiers were killed and injured, the war became more and more unpopular. Many people argued that it was wrong for the United States to get involved in a conflict that did not directly threaten the nation. Student protests took place across the country. At Kent State University in Ohio, four students were killed by National Guard troops as they protested the war.

Richard Nixon was elected president in 1968. As part of his campaign, he promised to end the war in Vietnam. Though a peace treaty was signed in 1973, it was still a few more years before the last troops came home. By the time the conflict was over, 56,000 Americans had died.

This photograph shows Richard Nixon leaving the White House by helicopter on the day of his resignation. His hands are raised, showing the "V for Victory" symbol—some people believe that was his way of insisting on his innocence in the Watergate scandal.

THE WATERGATE SCANDAL

Richard Nixon, a Republican, ran for reelection in 1972. One night in June during the campaign, burglars broke into the Democratic Party Headquarters at the Watergate Hotel in Washington, D.C. When investigators checked the burglars' backgrounds, they discovered that the burglars had links to the Republican Committee to Re-Elect the

Many people who were against the Vietnam War were unhappy that soldiers were being drafted, or called into service against their will. As the public began to think differently about the war, more and more people joined protest marches.

President (known as CREEP). It became clear that the Republicans were using "dirty tricks" such as stealing the other side's information to win the presidential campaign. As investigators dug deeper, they linked the Watergate break-in to government officials close to President Nixon. Many believed that Nixon himself had approved of the break-in. The Watergate scandal caused many people to lose faith in the government and to distrust the President. As a result, Richard Nixon resigned from the presidency in August 1974, the only president to have resigned from office.

Because of the work of environmentalist Rachel Carson and others, the government created the Environmental Protection Agency (EPA) in 1970 to clean up America's water, air, and land. Another environmental milestone happened in 1970: the first Earth Day.

A SHINY NEW APPLE

In 1976, Steve Jobs and Steve Wozniak founded the Apple Computer Company. Their first personal computer, called the Apple II, was an instant success. Apple was one of the first companies to attach a "mouse" to the personal computer.

PROTECTING THE ENVIRONMENT

Environmentalism, a movement to protect Earth, began in the early 1960s when a writer named Rachel Carson wrote a book called *Silent Spring.* Carson wrote about how the widespread spraying of a chemical called DDT was causing the deaths of songbirds across the United States. In the following years, people focused more on keeping America's land, air, and water clean, as well as on protecting endangered species and open lands. In the 1970s, the government passed laws to protect the environment, such as the Clean Air Act, the Clean Water Act, and the Endangered Species Act. These laws set rules for limiting air pollution from factories, created systems to clean up contaminated rivers and lakes, and preserved wild spaces.

NEW TECHNOLOGY

Just as new inventions had come on the scene at the end of the 19th century, new and exciting kinds of technology changed American life at the end of the 20th century, too. By the 1970s, companies such as IBM and Apple were creating early personal computers. For the first time, people used this technology to calculate numbers and create written documents. Compared to the computers people use now, the first such machines were large and slow. With their simple black-and-white screens and heavy processing units, they weren't nearly as handy or as portable as the computers of today.

Over the next few years, computer technology became more advanced and widespread. It also got much smaller. In the 1970s, hardly anyone thought about using computer chips in cars to give drivers directions, in televisions to save and record programs onto computers to be watched later, or in children's toys so they could speak and interact with their owners. Such ideas were considered science fiction. But as their use has grown and spread, computers have changed nearly every part of American life.

THE SPACE SHUTTLE

In 1972, President Nixon announced that the United States would begin to develop a new kind of spacecraft: the space shuttle. Before the space shuttle, American spaceships could make only a single trip into space—the ships were destroyed on the return home. The shuttle was special because it could return to space again and again for multiple missions. Though it launched into orbit like a rocket, the shuttle made horizontal landings just like an airplane. The first space shuttle, *Columbia,* went into orbit on April 12, 1981. American space shuttles have been used since then for research missions, to carry supplies to the International Space Station, and for repair missions, such as fixing the Hubble Space Telescope.

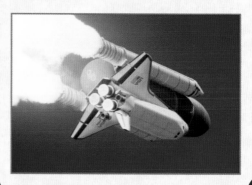

The Berlin Wall came down in November 1989, destroyed not by the government but by regular people. For many, the end of the wall symbolized the end of communism in Europe.

Ronald Reagan (*right*) was president of the United States from 1981 to 1989. During that time, he encouraged Soviet president Mikhail Gorbachev (*left*) to allow greater freedom to people living in the Soviet Union.

AMERICA IN WORLD AFFAIRS

The world has gotten smaller. This isn't because the size of the globe has actually changed. It just seems smaller because new technology such as computers, cell phones, and jets has made it easier for people in different countries to stay connected with each other. The countries of the world depend on each other to trade goods and to share information and resources.

That makes it difficult for the United States to be isolationist, as the Monroe Doctrine declared long ago. As a result, America has played an important role in world affairs in recent years.

THE WALL COMES DOWN

During much of the 1980s, the Soviet Union's leader was Mikhail Gorbachev. He began a series of talks with President Ronald Reagan. A period of openness, called *glasnost,* began in the Soviet Union.

Back in 1961, the Soviet government had built a wall separating parts of East Germany, which was under communist control, from West Germany. The wall was built to prevent people from escaping from the East to the West.

In 1989, Germans tore down the Berlin Wall and reunited East and West Germany. Then Poland, Hungary, Czechoslovakia, and Romania ended communist control in their countries. Finally, the Soviet Union broke into 15 separate countries. The Cold War had ended.

TROUBLE IN THE MIDDLE EAST

In 1990, the country of Iraq, led by a dictator named Saddam Hussein, invaded Kuwait, a tiny country with huge oil reserves. In January 1991, United Nations forces led by American generals declared war against Iraq. The Gulf War lasted six weeks. In that time, the United Nations forces drove Iraq's army out of Kuwait.

After the Gulf War, America continued to be involved in the Middle East, a part of the world where disagreements about land, resources, and religion have caused conflicts for years. While Bill Clinton was president in the late 1990s, he brought together Israeli and Palestinian leaders to try to resolve their differences.

The United States led a group of countries against Iraq after that country invaded its neighbor. Their combined forces pushed Iraq back into its own borders. In this photo, U.S. Marines take control of an abandoned Iraqi tank.

The terrorist attacks of September 11, 2001 were not the first time that terrorists had targeted the World Trade Center towers. In 1993, a car bomb damaged the towers, killing six people and injuring hundreds.

On September 11, 2001, terrorists hijacked four airplanes flying over the East Coast of the United States. The terrorists flew two of the airplanes into the World Trade Center towers in New York City and caused the towers to collapse. A third plane hit the Pentagon in Washington, D.C. The fourth plane crashed in Pennsylvania. As a result of the attacks, nearly 3,000 people died. Because of the events of September 11, the American government vowed to fight terrorism and protect America from future attacks.

The people responsible for the attacks were linked to al-Qaeda, a terrorist group based in the Middle East and Asia. In an effort to break up al-Qaeda in October 2001, American forces invaded Afghanistan, where many believed al-Qaeda's leader, Osama bin Laden, was hiding.

In 2003, American forces invaded Iraq. Their purpose was to remove Iraq's dictator, Saddam Hussein, and to set up a government where Iraqis could elect their own leaders. The U.S. government also claimed that Iraq was producing dangerous chemical and nuclear weapons, called weapons of mass destruction (or WMDs). Hussein was captured, but no weapons of mass destruction were found. American soldiers remained in Iraq while a new government was formed and tried to gain control of the country.

WHAT'S NEXT?

It would be fascinating to ask America's founders what they think of the United States today. How has it changed from its early days? How is it the same? And what will come next in America's story? It will be interesting to see how Americans face the challenges of the 21st century.

HURRICANE KATRINA
In late August 2005, Hurricane Katrina hit the Gulf Coast. It was one of the deadliest hurricanes in history. Scientists recorded the huge storm's winds at 175 miles per hour. The hurricane caused damage across Louisiana, Mississippi, and Alabama, especially along the coast. The greatest damage occurred in the city of New Orleans, where the storm caused water to break over the levees, or barriers, that separated Lake Pontchartrain from the city. Thousands of people evacuated, or left, the city. Over 80 percent of New Orleans flooded. Entire neighborhoods were destroyed, and nearly 2,000 people died. Though people are working hard to rebuild New Orleans, it will be a long time before the city has completely recovered.